Little Liza Jane and Her Sick FRIEND

ISBN 978-1-68526-993-7 (Hardcover)
ISBN 978-1-68526-992-0 (Digital)

Copyright © 2023 Lisa Marcotte
All rights reserved
First Edition

All rights reserved. No part of this publication may be reproduced, distributed, or transmitted in any form or by any means, including photocopying, recording, or other electronic or mechanical methods without the prior written permission of the publisher. For permission requests, solicit the publisher via the address below.

Covenant Books
11661 Hwy 707
Murrells Inlet, SC 29576
www.covenantbooks.com

Little Liza Jane and Her Sick FRIEND

Lisa Marcotte

The sun felt warm on this hot summer day.
Little Liza Jane was bored, but
her friend couldn't play.
Sitting under a tree with her chin on her knees,
Little Liza wondered, "How
sick could Linda be?"

It is summertime, and there is no school.
The days are so hot, and they
could be at the pool.

They could be playing in her backyard
or selling lemonade on the boulevard.

This was going to be a long, boring summer
unless Linda would quickly recover.
It must be lonely for Linda too,
all alone in her bedroom.

No friends to tell jokes to or laugh and play,
only lying in bed feeling awful all day.

What could Little Liza Jane do
to make Linda feel better?
Could she sing her a song, knit her a sweater?

Or perhaps she could even clean Linda's room,
be a little silly and dance with the broom.

This was hard for Little Liza Jane.
She didn't like seeing Linda sick and in pain.

Being silly might not be the
thing she should do,
maybe not even cleaning Linda's bedroom.

It's hard when someone isn't
feeling all that great.
You can't make them feel better,
and it is so hard to wait.

Linda's mom says she's not well
enough for visits from friends.
That makes me feel sad.
I hope she is well enough before summer ends.

"Hmmm," Little Liza Jane thought,
"just what could I do?
I've got a great idea! Oh yes, I do.
I'll write her cards and send her letters,
tell her how much I miss her and
hope she feels better soon."

Little Liza got out the crayons and the glue—
her scissors, paints, construction paper too.

Little Liza Jane felt so good
when she was all done.
Writing letters and making
cards was a lot of fun.

She could hardly wait to give
them to Linda's mother.
Each day for a week, one card after the other.

Each day, Little Liza Jane
would meet Mrs. Chan
at her back-door entry with a card in her hand.

On day number 4, when she met Mrs. Chan, she had a card for Little Liza Jane in her hand.

Little Liza Jane ran home and
lay down on her bed.
She was so excited to see what Linda's card said!

And so she read:
"Thank you, oh thank you, Little Liza Jane!
Your crafty cards and letters are
helping pass the days!
I miss you so much, and I'm thankful too
that I have a friend so kindhearted as you!
Your friend,
Linda Chan."

Little Liza Jane was surprised to see
that the card from Linda could
make her so happy.

What could you do to make
someone feel better too?

*Little Liza Jane is faceless because
she could be anyone of us.

About the Author

Lisa Marcotte is second to the youngest in a family of fifteen children. She is a mother of four and grandmother to six grandchildren. Lisa grew up in a few different places around the country, giving her many different life experiences. These experiences ultimately led her back to North Dakota, where she married a small-town farmer named Rob, and they have been happily married for thirty-seven years. They own and operate a farm in rural North Dakota, and with her grandchildren at her side while she is in the tractor, it is the perfect setting through which to write her stories.

The stories that Lisa writes are life lessons that she has learned or has taught her children and grandchildren. This story was written to encourage children to think of those who are sick and what they can do to make someone else feel better. It may even surprise children that they too will feel joy just for taking the time to make a card for a sick friend. She hopes that through this story, children will catch on to the idea of being kids who think of others, especially when they are sick.

Lisa wrote this story in dedication to Kinlee (one of her grandchildren) and in memory of her late friend Linda Chan.

CPSIA information can be obtained
at www.ICGtesting.com
Printed in the USA
BVHW011130140323
660405BV00007B/586